# Copycat Recipes Cookbook

*The Ultimate Guide to Make Your Favorite Fast Food Restaurant Dishes at Home*

**Jane Butler**

—

# Table of Contents

**CHAPTER 1: HAMBURGER RECIPES**...................................................**9**

1. McDonald's Egg McMuffin ...................................................9
2. Applebee's Quesadilla Burger .........................................11
3. White Castle Hamburgers ..............................................15
4. Pimento Cheese Burgers ...............................................17
5. Jack in the Box Mini Sirloin Burgers ...........................19
6. Culver's Butter Burgers...................................................21
7. Club Hamburger ............................................................23
8. Jack in the Box's Jumbo Jack .......................................25
9. K.F.C. Zinger Burger.......................................................27
10. Hardee's Mushroom Swiss Burger ..............................28
11. McDonalds Veggie Burger (Mc Aloo Tikki)..................31

**CHAPTER 2: FRIES AND NACHOS RECIPES**.............................**35**

1. Chili's Texas Cheese Fries................................................35
2. Joe's Crab Shack Crab Nachos .......................................37
3. Johnny Carino's Italian Nachos ...................................39
4. Outback Steakhouse Blooming Onion .........................41

**CHAPTER 3: SWEET, COOKIES AND ICE-CREAM RECIPES**......**43**

1. Pizza Hut Dessert Pizza .................................................43
2. T.J. Cinnamon's Cinnamon Rolls ..................................45
3. Mrs. Field's Applesauce-oatmeal Cookies ...................49
4. McDonald's Apple Pies...................................................51
5. Domino's Cinna Sticks ...................................................53

**CHAPTER 4: SNACK RECIPES** ...............................................**55**

1. T.G.I Friday's Pot Stickers .............................................55
2. Ruby Tuesday's Chicken Quesadillas............................59
3. Sparrow Chicken Frances ..............................................61
4. York Peppermint Patties ...............................................63
5. A&W's Coney Dog ...........................................................65
6. Golden Coral's Bourbon Street Chicken......................67
7. K.F.C.'s Grilled Chicken ................................................69
8. Luby Cafeteria's Fried Catfish.......................................71
9. Outback Steakhouse's Macaron Cheese .......................73
10. Mrs. Field's Pumpkin Harvest Cookies .......................75
11. Subway Sweet Onion Chicken Teriyaki Sandwich...........76

**CHAPTER 5: SAUCES, SLAWS AND DIPS RECIPES**....................**79**

1. Chick Fil Cole slaw ............................................................ 79

3. Don Pablo's Queso Dip ...................................................... 81

4. Joe's Crab Shack Crab Dip ................................................ 83

5. Outback Steakhouse Creole Marmalade Dipping Sauce ............... 85

6. T.G.I. Friday's Nine Layer Dip .......................................... 87

**CHAPTER 6: BEVERAGE RECIPES** ....................................... 89

1. Starbucks Pink Drink ........................................................ 89

2. Starbucks Hibiscus Refresher .............................................. 91

3. T.G.I. Friday's Long Island Iced Tea ................................... 93

4. Tommy Bahama Blue Hawaiian ............................................. 95

5. Tommy Bahama Calypso Sun ................................................ 97

6. Cinnabon Mocha Latte Chill .............................................. 99

7. Cinnabon Orange Icescape ................................................ 101

8. Dairy Queen Moo latte .................................................... 103

9. Dunkin Donuts Iced Coffee .............................................. 105

10. Houlihan's Houlis Fruit Fizz .......................................... 107

11. McDonald's Caramel Frappe ............................................ 109

**CONCLUSION** ................................................................ 111

# Introduction

I would like to thank and congratulate you for getting this book, Copycat Recipes.
People all over the world love to eat, enjoy and relax, especially in western countries. People love to go to restaurants to eat with their families, friends, and loved ones.

Whether you are a child or an adult, eating fast food outdoors has become a fast-growing trend. It is delicious and easy for everyone to enjoy. Many fast-food restaurants are opening all over the world due to the increasing demand of people.

Nowadays, hamburgers are people's go-to for fast food. If you live in America, you will know the value of burgers. It would not be wrong to say that America is the nation of burgers.
What if I told you that you can enjoy the famous fast-food dishes in the comfort of your own home?
Isn't that great?

Copied recipes truly inspire home cooking! Whether you are cooking for the whole family or entertaining with colleagues and friends. By following a copycat recipe, you will be able to serve an unforgettable meal that will bring joy to your family and friends.
This book mainly focuses on providing you with the replica recipes of the famous fast foods served all over the world by different fast-food restaurants.
Enjoy it!

# Chapter 1: Hamburger Recipes

## 1. McDonald's Egg McMuffin

**Preparation time: 40 minutes**

**Servings: 4**

**Difficulty: Moderate**

**Ingredients:**

- Four tablespoons softened butter has divided uses
- Four eggs
- Four English Muffins
- Half cup of water
- Four slices Canadian Bacon
- Four slices of American cheese

**Instructions:**

1. Split open English muffins, put them in a toaster and toast the English muffins.
2. Cook the Canadian bacon on both sides for around 1 to 2 minutes in two teaspoons of butter in a non-stick skillet over medium heat. The bacon should just start to brown.
3. Remove the English muffins from the toaster while the Canadian bacon is cooking, and spread softened butter on both halves.

4. Place one slice of Canadian bacon on the bottom of each English muffin.

5. In the same pan where you have fried the bacon, add about one tablespoon of butter.

6. Place the screw size of the quart-sized canning lids (or an egg ring can be used) in the skillet.

7. Spray non-stick spray onto the canning lid. Crack through each of the rings with an egg.

8. Break the yolk with a folk. Onto the skillet, pour about half a cup of water and put a cap on top. Cook until the eggs are set; this should take two minutes or so.

9. Remove the eggs from the rings gently, and put one egg on each Canadian bacon piece.

10. Cover each egg with a slice of American cheese and top the English muffin with the cheese.

11. Wrap the foil or parchment paper on each Mc Muffin egg. Before eating, wait for roughly 30 seconds.

# 2. Applebee's Quesadilla Burger

**Preparation time: 50 minutes**

**Servings: 4**

**Difficulty: Moderate**

**Ingredients:**

- Cheddar cheese Quesadillas
- 16 tortillas small, street taco sized
- Half cup Pico de Gallo
- One and a half cups shredded Cheddar cheese
- Burgers
- One and a half pounds ground chuck
- Half teaspoon of ground black pepper
- One teaspoon salt
- Mexican Ranch Sauce
- Half cup sour cream
- 1/4 cup salsa
- Half cup Ranch Salad Dressing
- One teaspoon taco seasoning
- Burger Toppings
- Two cups shredded iceberg lettuce
- Eight slices Applewood Bacon Cooked Crisp
- Eight slices of Pepper Jack cheese

## Instructions:

### Mexican Ranch Sauce

1. Combine the sour cream, ranch salad sauce, salsa, and taco seasoning in a shallow dish.
2. Stir to blend.

### Cheddar cheese Quesadillas

1. Preheat the oven to 200°C.
2. Divide the cheese into eight pieces to prepare eight quesadillas. On eight tortillas, put equivalent quantities of cheese. Place the remaining eight tortillas on top of the tortillas coated in cheese.
3. Cook the quesadillas for around two minutes on either side in a large non-stick skillet over medium heat. Quesadillas should have a golden-brown hue, and they should melt the cheese.
4. When you are frying the burgers, hold the quesadillas in the warm oven.

### Burgers

1. Combine the ground beef, salt, and black pepper in a dish. Stir to blend. Divide all four patties of beef.
2. Use the paper towel to clean the non-stick skillet and cook the burgers for 4 to 5 minutes on either side over medium heat.

### Build the Burgers

1. On a plate, put one quesadilla down, add one burger patty.

2. With two slices of Pepper Jack cheese and two slices of grilled bacon, a top burger patty.
3. Top the burger with Pico de Gallo, Shredded Cabbage, and Mexican Sauce.

# 3. White Castle Hamburgers

**Preparation time: 55 minutes**

**Servings: 4**

**Difficulty: Moderate**

## Ingredients:

- 12 dinner rolls
- Half cup water for beef
- One-pound ground beef
- Half teaspoon salts
- Dill hamburger slices
- One beef bouillon cube
- 3/4 cup onion diced
- Half cup water for onions

## Instructions:

1. Place the ground beef, salt, and water in a food processor. Process for a few seconds to mix water and salt with ground beef, and the meat can appear a little pasty.

2. Put plastic wrap on the bottom of an 11" x 13" jelly roll pan. Place the hamburger in the center and on top of the meat with another sheet of plastic wrap. Roll the hamburger to 1/4" thick.

3. Remove the plastic wrap, divide the meat into squares of 3" x 3" and leave the ground beef bits on the tray. You will have between 12 and 14 squares.

4. Perforate each slice with the end of a plastic straw five times, creating tiny steam holes for the beef. Cover the hamburger with plastic wrap and put it in the freezer until the meat is partly frozen.

5. In the frying pan, place the onions, beef bouillon, and half a cup of water. Sautee and stir onions on medium-low heat until they are clear; more water can be added if needed. Flip off the heat until the hamburger patties are ready to cook.

6. Turn the frying pan over medium-low heat when the beef patties are about to cook and apply enough water to the onions, only enough that the bottom of the frying pan is coated. Place the patties in a pan and cover them with a lid. Frying time is just a matter of moments away.

7. Turn and cook the patties until fully cooked but not dry. It should be moist. Place on top of a roll when hamburgers are done frying, add pickles, cover hamburgers so they can steam gently, or stick in the covering microwave for just a few seconds before ready to eat.

# 4. Pimento Cheese Burgers

**Preparation time: 40 minutes**
**Servings: 4**
**Difficulty: Moderate**

**Ingredients:**
**Pimento Cheese Spread**

- One tablespoon chopped pimento
- Four ounces sharp Cheddar cheese shredded
- A quarter cup of mayonnaise plus One tablespoon
- A quarter teaspoon of smoked Paprika
- 1/8 teaspoon Cayenne pepper

**Burger**

- One and a quarter pounds of ground chuck
- Half teaspoon ground black pepper
- One teaspoon salt
- Four hamburger buns
- Two teaspoons butter for buns

**Instructions:**
**Pimento Cheese Spread**

1. Combine the sliced strong Cheddar cheese, mayonnaise, Cayenne pepper, and paprika in a shallow bowl to cook the pimento cheese.

2. Stir to blend. Set yourself on the side while the burger is being made.

**Burger**

1. Combine ground chuck, salt, and pepper in a medium bowl. Divide the four parts of the beef. Press a tiny dimple into the center of the patties and turn each part into a disk about 1 inch wide. When frying, this dimple will help prevent your burgers from shrinking.

2. Over medium boil, heat an iron skillet. A teaspoon of butter is added to the skillet, and the buns are toasted. The typical skillet helps you heat two buns at one time (2 tops and two bottoms). Repeat this procedure until all the buns have been toasted.

3. Place the burger patties on the skillet, then turn the heat up to medium-high. Cook the burgers on the first side for 3 to 5 minutes. When you begin seeing the patty brown on the underside, the burgers will be able to turn. Flip the patties, then cook on the other side for an extra 3 to 5 minutes.

**Assembling**

1. Place the burger patties on the bottom buns to make the burger, cover the burger patty with one or two teaspoons of pimento cheese, and then top it with the top bun.

# 5. Jack in the Box Mini Sirloin Burgers

**Preparation time: 50 minutes**
**Servings: 4**
**Difficulty: Moderate**

## Ingredients:

- One-pound ground sirloin
- One teaspoon black pepper
- Half teaspoon seasoned salt
- Half onion sliced thin
- Four slices of American cheese
- Eight pickle slices
- Eight teaspoons ketchup
- One tablespoon peanut oil

## Instructions:

1. Place the ground sirloin, seasoned salt, and ground pepper together. Mix thoroughly. Thinly slice the onion and put it in a skillet of peanut oil. Slowly barbecue the onions. Don't brown the onions. Create 6 to 8 hamburger patties when the onions are almost transparent, make them thick (about 1/2 inch), and bring them into the hot plate.

2. Grill the hamburgers before rotating them for 4 to 5 minutes. Flip and cut the onions from the hamburgers. Assemble them with hamburger patties until they are

done. Bottom bun, pickle, patty beef, cheese, fried onions, ketchup, etc. Swiftly serve.

# 6. Culver's Butter Burgers

**Preparation time: 45 minutes**

**Servings: 4**

**Difficulty: Moderate**

## Ingredients:

- Four hamburger buns
- One tablespoon butter softened
- One-pound ground chuck
- Half teaspoon salts
- Half teaspoon black pepper
- Four slices of American cheese
- Four slices onion
- 8 - 12 dill pickles
- Eight tomato slices

## Instructions:

1. Over medium heat, heat a large skillet. Place the butter and whisk it around in the skillet. In the melting butter, lay the hamburger buns down. Allow about 60 seconds for the buns to toast. Remove the skillet buns.

2. Place four patties together and lay them in the skillet. On the hamburger patties, take the spatula and press down. Take a large soup covered in aluminum foil and press the skillet down with each meat patty. The burger patty will be fried on one side in about 2 minutes, so turn it over and do

the same on the other side. The other side will be cooked within about 60 seconds. With salt and pepper, season the patties.

3. Add cheese as you flip the burger over on the other side if you like to make cheeseburgers. Remove and put the meat patties on the bun. Add the desired toppings and enjoy your burger.

# 7. Club Hamburger

**Preparation time: 40 minutes**
**Servings: 4**
**Difficulty: Moderate**

## Ingredients:

- 1/4 cup finely chopped celery
- 1/4 cup chicken broth
- Two pounds ground top sirloin
- 1/4 cup bread crumbs
- Half teaspoon Worcestershire sauce
- 1/4 teaspoon nutmeg
- Salt and freshly ground pepper to taste
- Three tablespoons butter
- Four hamburger buns

## Instructions:

1. Combine celery and chicken broth in a shallow saucepan over meager heat; poach the celery for 20 minutes. Cool and drain.
2. Except for the sugar, add the celery with the remaining ingredients and blend well with your hands. Shape carefully into four broad patties, taking care not to make the meat more compact than required.
3. Heat the butter until the butter is amber in color in a large, heavy skillet over moderate heat.

4. Brown the burgers on each side for 6 minutes, then put the skillet for 6 to 8 minutes in a preheated 350F oven for medium-rare, a few extra minutes for better results.

# 8. Jack in the Box's Jumbo Jack

**Preparation time: 45 minutes**
**Servings: 1**
**Difficulty: Moderate**

**Ingredients:**
**Sauce:**

- One tablespoon mayonnaise
- Dash of lemon juice
- Pinch of onion powder
- Pinch of sugar
- One teaspoon ketchup

**Burger:**

- One sesame seed hamburger bun or plain hamburger bun, split in half
- One 4-ounce frozen beef patty
- Salt

**Toppings:**

- One and a half teaspoons chopped white onion
- Two slices of dill pickle
- Two large lettuce leaves
- Two tomato slices

**Instructions:**

1. Make the sauce by combining all the ingredients. Set aside, or refrigerate, covered, until ready to use.

2. Light a charcoal grill, or preheat an electric griddle to 400°F.

3. Toast the split hamburger bun on the grill, and set it aside. Place the frozen patty on the grill and cook for 4 to 5 minutes per side, salting both sides, turning once, and salting again after turning. Drain before putting on the bun.

4. Spread half the special sauce on the top half of the bun and add the onion, pickle slices, lettuce, and tomato.

5. Spread the remaining sauce on the bottom half of the bun and add the cooked patty. Cover with the top half of the bun and enjoy.

# 9. K.F.C. Zinger Burger

**Preparation time: 4 hours 20 minutes**

**Servings: 6**

**Difficulty: Hard**

## Ingredients:

- Three boneless chicken breasts (around half a kg)
- One teaspoon of pepper
- One teaspoon of salt
- Two tablespoons of Worcestershire sauce
- One teaspoon of Mustard powder or allspice powder
- Two tablespoons of Flour
- One Egg
- One and a half cups of Breadcrumbs
- Soft seeded burger buns
- Mayonnaise or K.F.C. Zinger Sauce

## Instructions:

1. Firstly, prepare your chicken breasts by chopping them if they are too large.
2. Afterward, marinate the chicken breasts with pepper, salt, mustard or allspice powder, and Worcestershire sauce. Leave the chicken overnight or at least 4 hours.
3. Then, prepare the batter, whisk together an egg and two tablespoons of water, and then set aside.

4. Put the marinated chicken breasts in flour and coat them generously.
5. Then dip them into the egg and then into the breadcrumbs until well coated.
6. Deep fry in hot oil the coated chicken breasts on medium to high heat until the breasts are golden brown and crispy.
7. Slice the buns in half and slightly toast them.
8. Then build the final burger, with the lettuce at the top, then the chicken and finally the mayonnaise or K.F.C. zinger sauce.
9. If you fancy a Cheesy Zinger, add sliced American cheese.

# 10. Hardee's Mushroom Swiss Burger

**Preparation Time: 40 minutes**

**Servings: 4**

**Difficulty: Moderate**

## Ingredients:

- One (10.75-ounce) can of Campbell's Golden Mushroom soup
- One small can have sliced mushrooms
- One teaspoon of Worcestershire sauce
- Half teaspoon of Accent seasoning
- Half teaspoon of Lawry's Seasoned Salt
- A quarter teaspoon of ground pepper
- One pound of hamburger
- Four slices of Swiss cheese

## Instructions:

1. Combine the mushroom broth, Worcestershire sauce and mushrooms.
2. Place the mixture over low heat in a small saucepan and let it boil.
3. Combine the hamburger with Accent, Seasoned Salt, and pepper.
4. Shape the hamburger into four patties and fry for 4-5 minutes per side in a skillet or grill until finished.

5. Place each patty on a bun and add the mushroom sauce and Swiss cheese.

# 11. McDonalds Veggie Burger (Mc Aloo Tikki)

**Preparation time: 45 minutes**
**Servings: 6**
**Difficulty: Moderate**

## Ingredients:

- Two Large potatoes
- 1/4 cup finely chopped onion
- 1/4 cup finely sliced carrots
- 1/4 cup sliced green beans
- 1/4 cup peas
- 3/4 teaspoon garlic powder
- One tablespoon oil
- Two tablespoons unsalted butter
- Two sliced tomatoes
- Milk

## Spices:

- 1/4 teaspoon turmeric powder
- Half teaspoon cumin powder
- One teaspoon paprika
- One teaspoon chat masala
- 3/4 teaspoon garlic powder
- Half teaspoon salts

**Batter:**

- Half cup all-purpose flour
- Four and a half tablespoons corn flour
- 1/4 cup cornmeal
- Half teaspoon salts
- One cup of water
- Half tablespoon oils
- Half tablespoon oils
- Half cup breadcrumbs

**Instructions:**

1. Start by boiling the potatoes for 15 minutes.
2. After 15 minutes, drain the potatoes
3. After draining, add a dash of milk and unsalted butter and mash the potatoes generously. Set aside.
4. Heat the oil and butter in a pan on medium to high heat.
5. Once it is hot, add in the onions and veggies and sauté for a couple of minutes.
6. Then add in the garlic powder and all other spices and mix well.
7. Lastly, add the mashed potato and blend properly, and simmer for a few more minutes.
8. Turn off the heat, dump the mixture into a mixing bowl and place it on one side for a few minutes to cool.
9. Blend in the bread crumbs after 10 minutes until the entire mixture is well mixed.

10. Cover the bowl and put it for 45 minutes in the fridge.

11. Build the batter by adding the all-purpose flour, corn flour, cornmeal and salt while the mixture is cooling.

12. Add a few dashes of water (only a little bit at a time) before mixing, then continue to stir until you hit a dense batter.

13. By adding oil and stirring together well, finish the batter.

14. Take the mixture out of the fridge after 45 minutes and roll the mixture into equal-sized balls. Flatten these balls into about half-inch thick patties.

15. In the batter, dip each patty and then cover it in bread crumbs.

16. First, heat a clean batch of oil over medium heat in a shallow pan. Until proceeding, wait until the oil is entirely up to temperature.

17. Next, put a few patties in the pan at a time and fry for around 2-3 minutes.

18. On the other hand, turn the patties over and cook for 2-3 minutes until both sides are golden brown.

19. Place each patty, until fried, on a paper towel.

20. Finally, assemble the burger by putting the patty on either bun and then stacking lettuce and tomatoes. To the top bun, add mayonnaise and near to full.

# Chapter 2: Fries and Nachos Recipes

## 1. Chili's Texas Cheese Fries

**Preparation time: 45 minutes**

**Servings: 4**

**Difficulty: Moderate**

### Ingredients:

- Half a (28-ounce) bag of frozen steak fries
- Four slices of bacon
- One (8-ounce) bag of shredded Cheddar cheese
- Jalapeño pepper slices, to taste
- Ranch salad dressing for dipping

### Instructions:

1. Spread the fries evenly over a cookie sheet and bake according to package instructions.
2. Line strips of bacon on another cookie sheet and bake for about 15–20 minutes, until crispy.
3. Remove them from the oven once the fries and bacon are done.
4. On top of the cooked fries, add a thick layer of cheese and jalapeños, then crumble the bacon on top.

5. Return to the oven and bake until the cheese melts for 8–10 minutes.

# 2. Joe's Crab Shack Crab Nachos

**Preparation time: 35 minutes**

**Servings: 4**

**Difficulty: Moderate**

## Ingredients:

- 16 baked tortilla chips
- One (8-ounce) package of chopped imitation crabmeat
- A quarter cup of sour cream
- A quarter cup of mayonnaise
- Two tablespoons chopped onion
- One cup shredded Cheddar cheese
- A quarter cup of a cup sliced black olives
- A quarter teaspoon of paprika

## Instructions:

1. Arrange tortilla chips on a baking sheet in a single layer.
2. Mix the crab, sour cream, mayonnaise, and onion in a bowl. Spoon on each chip with about one tablespoon.
3. Sprinkle on top of the chips, the cheese, olives, and paprika.
4. Bake for 6-8 minutes in a 350°F oven, or until the cheese melts.

# 3. Johnny Carino's Italian Nachos

**Preparation time: 30 minutes**

**Servings: 4**

**Difficulty: Moderate**

**Ingredients:**

- One (12-ounce) package of wontons
- One (1 pound) package of ground pork
- Three to four tablespoons olive oil
- Half cup Alfredo sauce
- One (6-ounce) package of grilled chicken pieces
- Two diced Roma tomatoes half cup sliced olives
- A quarter cup peperoncino pepper
- Jalapeño peppers, to taste
- One cup shredded mozzarella cheese

**Instructions:**

1. Preheat the oven to 400 degrees F.
2. On the diagonal, cut the wontons to form triangles.
3. In a sauté pan, cook pork for 10–12 minutes until brown.
4. Hurl triangles of wonton in olive oil and place on a baking sheet in a single layer.
5. Bake for 6 minutes or so, or until light brown. Remove from the oven and place for drainage on paper towels.
6. Pile the wontons and drizzle them with Alfredo sauce on a large serving platter.

7. Combine the wontons with pork, grilled chicken, tomatoes, olives, and peppers.

8. Top it with the mozzarella cheese. To melt the cheese, microwave for 1–2 minutes.

# 4. Outback Steakhouse Blooming Onion

**Preparation time: 2 hours 10 minutes**
**Servings: 1**
**Difficulty: Moderate**

**Ingredients:**
**Batter:**

- Four Vidalia or Texas Sweet Onions
- One-third cup cornstarch
- One and a half cups flour
- Two teaspoons garlic, minced
- Two teaspoons Paprika
- One teaspoon salt
- One teaspoon pepper
- 24 oz. beer
- Seasoned Flour
- Two cups flour
- Four teaspoons Paprika
- Two teaspoons garlic powder
- Half teaspoon peppers
- 1/4 teaspoon cayenne pepper

**Creamy Chili Sauce:**

- 1-pint Mayonnaise
- 1-pint Sour cream
- Half cup chili sauce

- Half teaspoon cayenne pepper

**Instructions:**

1. Until well blended, mix the cornstarch, flour, and seasonings.
2. Mix well, add beer.
3. "Cut off the top of the onion and peel about 3/4 ". Cut into 12 to 16 vertical wedges of onion, but do not cut through the bottom root.
4. Take about 1 inch of petals out of the center of the onion. Dip the onion into the seasoned flour and shake away the excess.
5. Separate the petals and dip to thoroughly coat them in the batter. Place gently in the fryer basket and deep-fry for one and a half minutes at 375 F to 400 F.
6. Turn over, and fry for one and a half more minute.
7. Drain on towels made of paper.
8. Place the onion upright in a shallow bowl and use a circular cutter or apple corer to remove the center core. With Creamy Chili Sauce, serve hot.

# Chapter 3: Sweet, Cookies and Ice-cream Recipes

## 1. Pizza Hut Dessert Pizza

**Preparation time: 55 minutes**
**Servings: 4-6**
**Difficulty: Moderate**

**Ingredients:**
**Pizza Crust:**

- One cup warm (105F) water
- Two cups flour
- One and a half tablespoons vegetable oil
- 3/4 cup cake flour
- One teaspoon salt
- 1/4 teaspoon active dry yeast

**Fruit Filling:**

- 1 – 21 oz. can pie filling (cherry, blueberry, or apple)

**Crumb Topping:**

- Half cup flours
- Half cup brown sugar
- Half cup quick oats
- Half cup firm butter or margarine
- One teaspoon cinnamon

**Vanilla Glaze:**

- Two cups powdered sugar
- Three tablespoon Milk
- One tablespoon Melted margarine or butter
- One teaspoon vanilla

**Instructions:**

1. Combine the yeast and hot water and leave for 3 minutes.
2. Add it in a large bowl to the other crust ingredients and knead for 10 minutes.
3. Cover and allow to rise for about 12 hours with plastic wrap.
4. Preheat oven to 500F.
5. Roll the dough until it is about the diameter of your 16-inch pizza pan on a floured surface.
6. Place the dough in the pan and shape it up to the edge. Brush with vegetable oil and use a fork to prick.
7. For 3 minutes, prebake. Remove from the oven and add pie filling to spread.
8. With a fork or a pastry blender, combine the crumb topping ingredients.
9. Spoon over the filling of the pie.
10. Put the pizza back in the oven and proceed to cook for 10-15 minutes or until the crust is light brown.
11. Remove and then drizzle vanilla glaze over it and serve.

# 2. T.J. Cinnamon's Cinnamon Rolls

**Preparation time: 1 hour**

**Servings: 12**

**Difficulty: Moderate**

**Ingredients:**

**Dough:**

- Two packs of active dry yeast
- Half cup warm water (105 to 115 degrees F)
- One-third cup sugar
- Half teaspoon sugars
- Four to five cups all–purpose flour, divided
- One teaspoon salt
- One cup milk, scalded and cooled to 110 degrees F
- One-third cup vegetable oil
- Two eggs, room temperature

**Filling:**

- Half cup butter or margarine softened
- 1 cup firmly packed brown sugar
- Half cup sugars
- Two tablespoons cinnamon

**Icing:**

- One cup confectioners' sugar
- Two to Three tablespoons warm milk

—

- One teaspoon vanilla

**Instructions:**

1. Dissolve the yeast in water with half a teaspoon of sugar for the dough. Let them
   stand for five minutes.
2. Combine three cups of rice, one-third cup sugar, and salt in a mixing dish. Gradually beat the milk, oil, eggs, and yeast mixture at low speed; beat until well blended. Beat in extra flour before the dough pulls away from the bowl's edges.
3. Knead the dough on a floured surface for 8-10 minutes, until smooth and elastic.
4. Move to an oiled top and put in an oiled tub.
5. Cover and let it rise until doubled in bulk, around 1 hour, in a safe, draft-free place.
6. Beat all ingredients together for the filling until smooth. Only put aside.
7. Oil 2 (9-inch) rectangular cake pans. Roll the dough into an 18 x 10-inch shaped rectangle on a thinly floured board. Spread with filling. From the longhand, roll firmly.
8. Split into 14 slices (1 1/4 of an inch). In the center of each plate, place one roll cut side up. Arrange the remaining rolls around the central roll in a circle of 6.
9. Cover and let rise for 30 to 40 minutes before doubled in bulk.

10. Preheat the oven to 350°C. Bake until golden brown, 25 to 30 minutes. Cool for 10 minutes in pots. Invert to cool on wire shelves, then invert again.

11. Whisk all ingredients until smooth for the icing. Drizzle over refrigerated rolls.

# 3. Mrs. Field's Applesauce-oatmeal Cookies

**Preparation time: 1 hour**
**Servings: 48 cookies**
**Difficulty: Moderate**

**Ingredients:**
- Two and a half cups all-purpose flour
- One cup quick-cooking rolled oats
- Half teaspoon salts
- One teaspoon baking soda
- One teaspoon ground cinnamon
- A quarter teaspoon ground clove
- Two teaspoons grated lemon zest
- One cup packed dark brown sugar
- One to two tablespoons (One and a half sticks) unsalted butter, softened
- One large egg
- Half cup unsweetened applesauce
- Half cup honeys
- One cup finely chopped peeled apple
- One cup of raisins
- Half cup quick-cooking rolled oats (optional)

**Instructions:**

1. Preheat the oven to 300°F.

2. Combine the flour, 1 cup of rolled oatmeal, salt, baking soda, cinnamon, cloves and lemon zest in a big bowl.

3. Whisk together all so that all the dry products are spread equally.

4. Beat the brown sugar and the butter in another big bowl until the mixture is light and fluffy. Add the egg, then the applesauce, then the butter, with the mixer working.

5. Add the dry ingredients gently, 1 cup at a time, combining well with each addition; add the chopped apple and raisins, then blend until just blended.

6. Drop onto ungreased baking sheets with rounded tablespoonfuls about 1 inch away. If needed, sprinkle with half the cup of rolled oats. Bake until the bottoms are golden, 20 to 25 minutes. Move to cool to wire shelves.

# 4. McDonald's Apple Pies

**Preparation time: 1 hour**

**Servings: 8**

**Difficulty: Moderate**

## Ingredients:

- One Granny Smith Apple
- One red apple
- Three tablespoons butter
- Three tablespoons brown sugar
- Half teaspoon ground cinnamon
- 1/4 teaspoon nutmeg
- 1/4 teaspoon allspice
- 1/4 teaspoon vanilla extract
- One teaspoon lemon juice
- 1/4 teaspoon salt
- Two sheets Puff Pastry cut into 8-inch squares

## Instructions:

1. Dice apples into tiny parts. Place the apples, over medium heat, in a jar. Add the butter, brown sugar, cinnamon, nutmeg, allspice, vanilla extract, salt, and lemon juice to the pot. Cook the apples for 10 to 12 minutes or until they are tender.

2. According to box instructions, defrost the puff pastry. Break the puff pastry into eight triangles. To one hand of

each of the triangles, spoon one heaping tablespoon of cooked apples. Brush water on the side of the edge of each square and fold the squares on top of each other. Crimp the sides together with a fork.

3. To cover the bottom three inches, apply ample oil to your cooking utensil. Then heat the oil to 350 degrees F. When you put a small piece of dough into the oil, the oil will be ready, and it will cook fast. Cook two pies at a time, on either hand, for about 1 minute. Remove until both sides are golden brown; put pies on a wire rack when pies are removed from hot oil to drain excess oil; if you want to keep the pies soft, retain until you are ready to serve in a 200-degree oven.

# 5. Domino's Cinna Sticks

**Preparation time: 45 minutes**

**Servings: 12**

**Difficulty: Moderate**

## Ingredients:

- One package of refrigerated pizza dough
- A quarter cup melted margarine
- Half cup sugars
- Two teaspoons cinnamon

## Icing:

- One pound of powdered sugar
- One tablespoon milk
- One tablespoon melted butter
- A quarter teaspoon of vanilla extract

## Instructions:

1. Preheat the oven to 350°F.
2. Roll the dough out of the pizza into a long rectangle.
3. The melted margarine is rubbed over the dough. In a shallow dish, combine the sugar and cinnamon.
4. Over the pizza dough, spray the mixture liberally. Halve the dough and then slice it into tiny sticks.
5. Place the dough on a cookie sheet that is lightly greased and bake it for 15 minutes.

6. Combine all the icing ingredients in a little bowl. For dipping, serve icing alongside the sticks.

# Chapter 4: Snack Recipes

## 1. T.G.I Friday's Pot Stickers

**Preparation time: 45 minutes**

**Servings: Eight dozen**

**Difficulty-Moderate**

**Ingredients:**

**Dough:**

- Two and a half cups flour
- Half teaspoon salts
- One cup of hot water
- One tablespoon shortening or oil

**Filling:**

- One-pound ground pork
- Two tablespoons of soy sauce
- One tablespoon sesame oil
- One teaspoon grated ginger
- Pinch of sugar
- Salt and pepper to taste
- Three green onions, chopped
- One egg
- One tablespoon corn starch
- One can water chestnuts, finely chopped

- One clove garlic, minced

**Dipping Sauce:**
- Half cup soy sauce
- 1/4 cup white vinegar
- One teaspoon chili oil
- One green onion, chopped

## Instructions:

1. In a bowl, mix the rice, salt, hot water and shortening and proceed it to be a smooth dough. Allow the dough, wrapped, to rest for 20 minutes. Combine the ingredients for the filling.
2. Combine the ingredients for the dipping sauce.
3. Roll out about 1/8 thick of the dough. For cutting out 3-inch triangles, use a biscuit cutter or a glass.
4. Rub over the circles with a little water and put in the middle around two teaspoons of filling. Fold the circles in half and press to close, making sure all air is pushed out.
5. Stand the dumplings up on the folded side and press slightly so that they stand up nice.
6. Bring a pot of salted water to a boil to cook, and boil the dumplings until cooked for about 5 minutes. Drain thoroughly.
7. Heat a skillet with about two tablespoons of oil and fry just one side of the dumplings until they are well browned.

8. Drain on towels made of cloth. Using the dipping sauce to serve it

# 2. Ruby Tuesday's Chicken Quesadillas

**Preparation time: 55 minutes**

**Servings: 4**

**Difficulty: Moderate**

**Ingredients:**

- 5 oz. chicken breast
- Italian Dressing
- 12-inch flour tortilla
- Margarine
- One cup shredded Monterey jack/cheddar cheese
- One tablespoon of tomatoes, diced
- One tablespoon of jalapeno peppers, diced
- Cajun Seasoning (to taste)
- Half cup shredded lettuce
- 1/4 cup diced tomatoes
- Sour Cream
- Salsa

**Instructions:**

1. In a bowl, put Italian dressing generously to coat the chicken,
2. Put the chicken breast in the bowl; let marinate, store in the fridge for 30 minutes.
3. Grill the marinated chicken in a lightly oiled pan until cooked.

4. Split and set aside into 3/4" pieces."

5. Brush one side of the margarine tortilla and put over medium heat in a frying pan.

6. Add cheese, one tablespoon of tomatoes, peppers, and Cajun seasoning to one half of the tortilla, in that order.

7. Be sure that it stretches to the edge of the half. Cover with diced chicken, fold on top of the empty tortilla side and turn over in the pan so that the chicken is cheese on top of the chicken. Cook until it's all really warm.

8. Lift from the pan to the serving dish and cut one side of the plate into six even wedges. Lettuce, on the other hand, topped with 1/4 cup of tomatoes and topped with sour cream.

9. In a little bowl on the side, serve your favorite salsa.

# 3. Sparrow Chicken Frances

**Preparation time: 45 minutes**

**Servings: 4**

**Difficulty: Moderate**

**Ingredients:**

- Five boneless 5 oz. Chicken breasts
- Five eggs
- Three oz. Romano cheese
- One teaspoon dried parsley
- One cup flour
- Pinch of white pepper
- One cup chicken stock
- Half pound butter
- Juice from two lemons
- One and a half cup of oil
- Lemon slices for garnish
- Chopped fresh parsley for garnish

**Instructions:**

1. Pound flat the chicken breasts and cut them in two. And put aside.
2. Scramble in a mixing dish with the eggs. Garnish with Romano cheese, parsley, and white pepper. Mix and put aside.
3. In a wide shallow dish, put the flour.

4. Heat oil over low heat in a pan. Dip a corner of a chicken piece in oil, check the temperature. Oil is ready if it cooks steadily.
5. Coat a slice of chicken on both sides with flour.
6. Dip the chicken into the egg mixture, making sure the egg is coated with all the starch. Drip off the excess egg then put the chicken in the hot oil.
7. With four more bits, repeat. Fry each side of the chicken until the color is light blond. Remove from the oil and remain warm on a serving tray.
8. Repeat for the other bits of chicken.
9. Bring the stock of chicken to a light boil. Add butter when melted, stirring constantly. Add the lemon juice and simmer for one minute while constantly stirring.
10. Pour the sauce over the chicken and garnish with the chopped fresh parsley and the lemon slices.

# 4. York Peppermint Patties

**Preparation time: 50 minutes**

**Servings: 4**

**Difficulty: Moderate**

**Ingredients:**

- One (14–ounce) can Eagle Brand Sweetened Condensed Milk
- One tablespoon peppermint extract
- Green or red food coloring, optional
- Six cups confectioners' sugar
- Additional confectioners' sugar
- One 16 oz. bag semi–sweet chocolate chips.

**Instructions:**

1. If needed, blend Eagle Brand, extract, and food coloring in a large mixer bowl.
2. Add 6 cups sugar; beat until smooth and well blended at low speed. Turn the mixture sprinkled with confectioner's sugar onto the surface.
3. To shape a smooth ball, knead gently. Form into balls measuring 1 inch, on wax paper-lined baking sheets, set 2 inches apart.
4. Flatten each ball into a patty of around one and a half inches. Let it dry for 1 hour or longer; turn over and let it dry for 1 hour or more.

5. Melt the chocolate chips in a microwave set on high for 2 minutes.
6. Stir halfway into the heating cycle. Thoroughly melt, but don't overheat.
7. A double-boiler over low heat may also be used to melt the chocolate chips. Immerse each patty in warm chocolate with a fork.
8. Invert onto baking sheets lined with wax paper; let stand until solid. Hold it wrapped in the refrigerator or at room temperature.

# 5. A&W's Coney Dog

**Preparation time: 1 hour**
**Servings: 4**
**Difficulty: Moderate**

**Ingredients:**
**Coney Island Chili Dog Sauce:**

- One-pound ground chuck
- One teaspoon salt
- A quarter teaspoon pepper
- One 6-ounce can of tomato paste
- One cup of water
- One tablespoon sugar
- One tablespoon yellow mustard
- One tablespoon of onion flakes
- Two teaspoons chili powder
- One teaspoon Worcestershire sauce
- Half teaspoon celery seeds
- Three-fourth teaspoon ground cumin

**Coney Dog:**

- One 2-ounce Sabert beef frankfurter (7Half inches long)
- One regular hot dog bun
- One tablespoon chopped onion
- One and a half teaspoons shredded Cheddar cheese

---

## Instructions:

1. Make the chili dog sauce. Sauté the ground chuck in a dry saucepan, crumbling it as it browns. Add the remaining sauce ingredients. Let the mixture simmer, occasionally stirring, until it thickens, 30 to 40 minutes.

2. Let cool and refrigerate in a covered container until ready to use. Gently reheat Three tablespoons, the portion needed for one serving.

3. Boil water in a saucepan, add the frankfurter, cover the pan, remove it from the heat, and let the hot dog sit for 10 minutes.

4. Microwave the bun for 10 seconds, remove the frankfurter from the water with tongs and put it in the bun.

5. Pour the warm chili sauce over the hot dog and garnish with the onion and cheese, if desired.

# 6. Golden Coral's Bourbon Street Chicken

**Ready in about: 1 hour**
**Servings: 4**
**Difficulty: Moderate**

## Ingredients:

- Half cup soy sauce
- Half cup packed dark brown sugar
- Half teaspoon garlic powder
- One teaspoon ground ginger
- Two tablespoons onion flakes
- Half cup Jim Beam bourbon, or another brand of your choice
- One-pound chicken leg or thigh meat, cut into bite-size pieces
- Two tablespoons white wine

## Instructions:

1. Whisk together the soy sauce, brown sugar, garlic powder, ginger, onion flakes, and Bourbon.
2. Pour over the chicken pieces in a bowl and marinate in the refrigerator for 4 hours, stirring occasionally.
3. Preheat the oven to 350°F.

4. Transfer the chicken to a baking pan and arrange in a single layer. Pour any marinade left in the bowl over the chicken pieces and bake for 1 hour, stirring and basting with the marinade about every 10 minutes.

5. When the chicken is cooked through, transfer it to a plate and keep warm. If you used a metal baking pan, place it over a stovetop burner and deglaze the pan with the white wine, scraping up all the browned bits and the pan juices over medium-low heat. If you used glass or ceramic dish, transfer the dish's contents to a skillet and add the white wine.

6. Add the chicken to the baking pan or skillet and simmer for 5 minutes; serve warm.

# 7. K.F.C.'s Grilled Chicken

**Preparation time: 1 hour**

**Servings: 4-5**

**Difficulty: Moderate**

**Ingredients:**

**Brine:**

- A quarter cup of salt
- One tablespoon accent flavor enhancer
- One two and a half to three-pound chicken, cut into eight pieces

**Dry rub seasoning mix:**

- Two teaspoons of all-purpose flour
- A quarter teaspoon of salt
- A three-fourth teaspoon of chicken bouillon powder
- A quarter teaspoon of beef bouillon powder
- A quarter teaspoon dried marjoram
- A quarter teaspoon coarsely ground pepper
- A quarter teaspoon dried rosemary, crushed
- A quarter teaspoon dried basil
- Pinch of dried oregano
- Pinch of garlic powder
- A quarter cup of vegetable oil
- A quarter teaspoon of liquid smoke
- A quarter teaspoon of soy sauce

## Instructions:

1. Create some brine. Dissolve the salt and the Accent flavor enhancer in the water in a container big enough to hold 8 cups of water and all the chicken bits. Attach the bits of chicken, make sure that they are submerged.

2. Refrigerate for 2 hours at the very least. The brining would ensure that it is moist and tender for the fried chicken.

3. Combine all the dry rub ingredients and place them until ready to use in a sealed jar.

4. Preheat the oven to 350°F.

5. Combine and set aside the cooking oil, liquid smoke, and soy sauce.

6. Drop the brine from the chicken and pat it off. Throw the brine dry. Brush the mixture of vegetable oil on both sides of each chicken piece, and then sprinkle the dry rub evenly.

7. Heat a grill or a grill pan with elevated ridges, and cook each piece of chicken just long enough on both sides to create distinctive grill marks.

8. Move the chicken to a baking sheet and roast in the oven for at least 20 minutes on each side, rotating once until golden brown and cooked through.

# 8. Luby Cafeteria's Fried Catfish

**Preparation time: 45 minutes**
**Servings: 6**
**Difficulty: Moderate**

## Ingredients:

- A quarter cup lemon juice
- Two teaspoons Worcestershire sauce
- Two cups all-purpose flour
- A quarter cup paprika
- Two tablespoons seasoned salt
- Vegetable oil for frying
- Six 7- to 8-ounce catfish fillets
- Lemon slices or wedges, for garnish
- Fresh parsley sprigs for garnish

## Instructions:

1. Whisk together 2 cups of water, lemon juice, and the Worcestershire sauce in a shallow bowl.
2. In another shallow bowl, combine the flour with the paprika and seasoned salt.
3. In a heavy skillet, heat 1 inch of vegetable oil (or enough to cover the fillets) to 350°F. Dip each fillet first in the lemon juice mixture, then in the flour blend. Shake off any excess flour.

4. Fry the fillets, one at a time, turning once until the coating is crispy and golden brown. Drain on paper towels.

5. Serve each fillet garnished with lemon and parsley.

# 9. Outback Steakhouse's Macaron Cheese

**Preparation time: 40 minutes**
**Servings: 2-3**
**Difficulty: Moderate**

## Ingredients:

- Three tablespoons butter
- Two tablespoons all-purpose flour
- One and a half cups milk
- A quarter teaspoon salt
- 1/8 teaspoon paprika
- 8 ounces Velveeta cheese, cubed
- 12 ounces medium rigatoni pasta, cooked according to the package Instructions

## Instructions:

1. Melt the butter in a medium saucepan and whisk in the flour, stirring to thicken. Do not let the butter brown.
2. Whisk in the milk, salt, and paprika, then the Velveeta cubes, incorporating them all until the sauce thickens. If it seems too thick, add a little more milk.
3. Add the cooked pasta to the sauce and serve warm.

# 10. Mrs. Field's Pumpkin Harvest Cookies

**Preparation time: 45 minutes**

**Servings: 48 cookies**

**Difficulty: Moderate**

## Ingredients:

- One cup pecan halves and pieces
- Two and a quarter cups all-purpose flour
- One teaspoon pumpkin pie spice
- Half teaspoon baking soda
- One and a Half cups packed dark brown sugar
- Half pound (2 sticks) unsalted butter, softened
- One cup pumpkin puree one tablespoon vanilla extract
- Two large eggs
- 10 ounces white chocolate, coarsely chopped

## Instructions:

1. Preheat the oven to 300°F.
2. Toast the pecans. Spread the nuts out on a baking sheet and bake until they begin to color, stirring often. Set aside to cool.
3. In a bowl, combine the flour, pumpkin pie spice, and baking soda.
4. In a large bowl, beat the brown sugar and butter until light and fluffy. Gradually beat in the pumpkin puree, vanilla

extract, and the eggs, one at a time. Add the dry ingredients, one cup at a time, until just combined—do not overmix. Stir in the chocolate and pecans.

5. Drop by rounded tablespoonfuls, about 2 inches apart, onto ungreased baking sheets. Bake for 20 to 25 minutes, then transfer to wire racks to cool.

# 11. Subway Sweet Onion Chicken Teriyaki Sandwich

**Preparation time: 50 minutes**
**Servings: 1**
**Difficulty: Moderate**

**Ingredients:**

- One boneless, skinless chicken breast
- A quarter cup Lawry's teriyaki marinade
- One bakery-fresh sub roll
- Sliced vegetables of your choice
- Sweet Onion Sauce
- Half cup light corn syrup
- One tablespoon red wine vinegar
- One tablespoon minced white onion
- Two tablespoons white vinegar
- One teaspoon brown sugar
- One teaspoon balsamic vinegar
- A quarter teaspoon lemon juice
- 1/8 teaspoon salt
- 1/8 teaspoon poppy seeds
- Pinch of cracked black pepper
- Pinch of garlic powder

**Instructions:**

- Place and marinate the chicken breast in a zip-top bag. In the refrigerator, marinate the chicken for 30 minutes.
- In a shallow microwave-safe dish, combine all the sauce ingredients. Heat until the mixture boils for 1–2 minutes.
- Stir thoroughly, cover and let cool.
- On a George Foreman barbecue or stovetop grill pan, cook the chicken. Cut into slices of 1/4″.
- Place the chicken on the roll of a subway. Whatever veggies you like, add them.
- Pour over the chicken and vegetables with the hot onion sauce.

# Chapter 5: Sauces, Slaws and Dips Recipes

## 1. Chick Fil Cole slaw

**Preparation time: 35 minutes**
**Servings: 4**
**Difficulty: Moderate**

**Ingredients:**

- Six cups of shredded cabbage
- 1/4 cup sugar
- One cup of shredded carrots
- Half teaspoons salt
- 1/4 teaspoons pepper
- Half cup milks

**Dressing:**

- Half cup mayonnaise
- Half teaspoons celery seed
- Two to three drops of hot sauce
- Three tablespoons dry minced onion
- Half cup buttermilk

**Instructions:**

1. Mix all the ingredients except those of the dressing.
2. Chill 15 minutes.

3. Afterward, combine all the ingredients of the dressing separately.

4. Mix the dressing well with cabbage. Chill. Allow flavors to blend for several hours before serving.

# 3. Don Pablo's Queso Dip

**Preparation time: 45 minutes**

**Servings: 6-8**

**Difficulty: Moderate**

**Ingredients:**

- Three tablespoons butter
- One cup chopped onion
- One 20-ounce can Rote diced tomatoes with green chiles, with juice
- One 14.5-ounce can have stewed tomatoes, chopped, with juice
- Two pounds of processed cheese such as Velveeta, cubed
- One pound of sharp Cheddar cheese, cubed
- Tortilla chips, for serving

**Instructions:**

1. Heat the butter in a large saucepan and lightly sauté the onion until soft. Add both cans of tomatoes and simmer until thickened.
2. Add the cheeses to the tomato mixture and stir over medium heat until the cheese is melted and smooth.
3. Let cool, then refrigerate overnight in a covered container. Gently reheat before serving with tortilla chips.

# 4. Joe's Crab Shack Crab Dip

**Preparation time: 30 minutes**
**Servings: 4**
**Difficulty: Moderate**

## Ingredients:

- One (5-ounce) can have drained crab meat
- One (8-ounce) package softened cream cheese
- Three tablespoons heavy whipping cream
- Two teaspoons diced onion
- Two teaspoons diced red pepper
- Two teaspoons diced green pepper
- Two teaspoons diced tomato
- Two teaspoons diced green onion
- Two teaspoons white wine one tablespoon Parmesan cheese
- Half teaspoon Old Bay seasoning
- Dash of Tabasco sauce, to taste

## Instructions:

1. Combine all the ingredients in a shallow microwave-safe dish.
2. Microwave for 4 minutes on medium power.
3. Remove from the oven, blend, and eat with chips or toast.

# 5. Outback Steakhouse Creole Marmalade Dipping Sauce

**Preparation time: 35 minutes**
**Servings: Half cup**
**Difficulty: Moderate**

## Ingredients:

- Half cup orange marmalade
- Two teaspoons Grey Pompon mustard
- One teaspoon white horseradish sauce
- Dash Tabasco sauce
- Salt, to taste

## Instructions:

1. Put all the ingredients listed together in a small bowl

2. Let it cool down in the refrigerator for at least 30 minutes.

3. Serve chilled.

# 6. T.G.I. Friday's Nine Layer Dip

**Preparation time: 40 minutes**

**Servings: 4**

**Difficulty: Moderate**

## Ingredients:

- Two strips of diced bacon
- One (16-ounce) can of plain refried beans
- One (1.25-ounce) package of taco seasoning
- Half cup sour cream
- Three-fourth cup shredded Cheddar cheese
- Three-fourth cup guacamole
- One-third cup diced tomatoes
- Two tablespoons finely sliced green onions
- Two tablespoons sliced black olives

## Instructions:

1. In a pan, cook the bacon. Remove the refried beans and add to the bacon and drippings to cook together.
2. Stir regularly and simmer for 15 minutes at low temperatures.
3. Set aside and mix the taco seasoning with sour cream.
4. Place on a plate the refried beans and layer 1'' thick. Gather half a cup of cheese on top of the beans.
5. A half-cup of the sour cream mixture is the next coat. Cover with three-forth cup guacamole.

6. Garnish with sliced tomatoes, carrots, black olives and a quarter cup of cheese.

# Chapter 6: Beverage Recipes

## 1. Starbucks Pink Drink

**Preparation time: 35 minutes**
**Servings: 1**
**Difficulty: Easy**

**Ingredients:**
**Simple Syrup**

- One cup of water
- Two cups of sugar
- Drink preparation
- One tea bag Tazo Passion Herbal Tea
- Two tablespoons simple syrup
- Half cup white grape juice
- Three tablespoons coconut milk
- Two tablespoons chopped fresh strawberries

**Instructions:**
**Simple Syrup**

1. Put one cup of water and two cups of sugar in a saucepan to prepare a basic syrup.

2. Just until the mixture starts to simmer, heat to medium-high; stir regularly as the syrup heats. Until the sugar has melted, stir.
3. Before adding it to the cocktail, let the syrup cool.
4. Tea Preparation
5. Prepare one bag of tea by adding 8 ounces of boiling water.
6. Allow the tea too steep for five minutes.
7. Allow the tea to cool down.
8. Building the Pink Drink
9. Add Two tablespoons of simple syrup to a glass and add half a teacup to the glass.
10. Add half a cup of white grape juice to the glass. Stir well.
11. Add ice to the glass. Add three tablespoons of coconut milk and mix gently.
12. Add chopped strawberries and serve immediately.

# 2. Starbucks Hibiscus Refresher

**Preparation time: 35 minutes**

**Servings: 2**

**Difficulty: Easy**

**Ingredients:**

**Simple Syrup**

- One cup of sugar
- One cup of water
- Tea Ingredients
- One green tea bag
- One hibiscus tea bag
- Two cups of water
- 1/4 cup white grape juice
- Two tablespoons simple syrup or to taste
- 1/4 cup frozen berries

**Instructions:**

**Simple Syrup**

1. Mix the water and sugar in a saucepan, making a basic syrup. Bring it to a boil and cook for 2 minutes or until the sugar dissolves.
2. Remove from heat before use, and allow to cool.
3. Tea Assembly

4. Using those two cups of water to brew the green and hibiscus tea. Allow for 5 minutes to steep and then allow to cool.

5. In a bottle, pour the cooled tea, the pure cooled syrup and the white grape juice. Stir to blend. Top with frozen berries of choice and frost.

# 3. T.G.I. Friday's Long Island Iced Tea

**Preparation time: 25 minutes**
**Servings: 1**
**Difficulty: Easy**

**Ingredients:**

- Half ounce gins
- Half ounce vodka
- Half ounce rum
- Half ounce Triple Sec
- 2 ounces sweet and sour mix
- Splash of cola

**Instructions:**

1. Mix all the ingredients in a shaker.
2. Pour over ice and top with cola.

# 4.Tommy Bahama Blue Hawaiian

**Preparation time: 45 minutes**

**Servings: 1**

**Difficulty: Easy**

## Ingredients:

- One part of (one-shot) Tommy Bahama White Sand Rum
- One part of Blue Curacao
- Two parts pineapple juice
- One-part coconut cream
- Crushed ice
- Pineapple slice, for garnish
- Maraschino cherry, for garnish

## Instructions:

1. In a mixer with a scoop of crushed ice, pour the rum, Blue Curacao, pineapple juice and coconut milk. Blend until perfectly smooth. Pour yourself into a bottle.
2. Garnish with a slice of fresh pineapple and a maraschino cherry.

# 5. Tommy Bahama Calypso Sun

**Preparation time: 20 minutes**

**Servings: 1**

**Difficulty: Easy**

### Ingredients:

- Two ounces Tommy Bahama Golden Sun Rum
- Two ounces pineapple juice
- One ounce of fresh orange juice
- One-ounce Coco Lopez

### Instructions:

1. Mix all ingredients over ice in a hurricane glass

# 6. Cinnabon Mocha Latte Chill

**Preparation time: 25 minutes**

**Servings: 2**

**Difficulty: Easy**

## Ingredients:

- One cup cold strong coffee
- One cup half-and-half
- Half cup chocolate syrup
- Whipped cream for garnish

## Instructions:

1. Make double-strength coffee in your coffee maker by adding half the water suggested by the manufacturer. Allow the brewed coffee to chill in the refrigerator for at least an hour.
2. Combine all ingredients listed in a small pitcher and stir well.
3. Pour over ice in 2 (16-ounce) glasses
4. Top with whipped cream.

# 7. Cinnabon Orange Icescape

**Preparation time: 20 minutes**

**Servings: 2**

**Difficulty: Easy**

**Ingredients:**

- Three cups crushed ice
- One cup of water
- 2/3 cup orange juice
- Half cup half-and-half
- Three tablespoons Tang orange drink mix

**Instructions:**

1. Pour all the ingredients into a blender.

2. Mix on high speed until smooth and creamy.

3. Serve in 2 (16-ounce) glasses.

# 8. Dairy Queen Moo latte

**Preparation time: 25 minutes**

**Servings: 2**

**Difficulty: Easy**

## Ingredients:

- Three tablespoons sugar
- 1/8-ounce teaspoons salt
- One cup strong coffee
- Half cup half-and-half cream
- Six big ice cubes
- Two cups vanilla ice cream
- A half cup milk
- Three tablespoon chocolate or caramel syrup and Whipped cream for garnish

## Instructions:

1. Mix the coffee, milk, half-and-half, sugar and salt in a blender till to dissolve the sugar.

2. Add ice cream, and chocolate or caramel syrup in a mixer.

3. Then blend until smooth and creamy.

4. Add the ice cubes, and use the pulse (ice feature) to crush the ice into tiny bits.

5. Pour into two glasses (16-ounce) and finish with whipped cream and a drizzle chocolate or caramel syrup.

# 9. Dunkin Donuts Iced Coffee

**Preparation time: 25 minutes**

**Servings: 1**

**Difficulty: Easy**

## Ingredients:

- One tablespoon sugar
- Four ice cubes
- 2/3 cup cold coffee
- 2/3 cup milk

## Instructions:

1. Put the sugar in a large glass.

2. Drop-in ice cubes.

3. Pour coffee over the ice and add milk.

4. Stir until the sugar has dissolved.

# 10. Houlihan's Houlis Fruit Fizz

**Preparation time: 20 minutes**
**Servings: 2**
**Difficulty: Easy**

### Ingredients:

- One (12-ounce) can of cold Sprite
- Half cup cold pineapple juice
- A quarter cup cold orange juice
- One cup cold cranberry juice

### Instructions:

1. Mix all of the ingredients mentioned above in a pitcher.

2. Pour into two glasses over ice.

3. Be sure all of the ingredients are cold when combined

# 11. McDonald's Caramel Frappe

**Preparation time: 5 minutes**

**Servings: 2**

**Difficulty: Easy**

## Ingredients:

- Two cups Ice
- Half cup Milk
- Half cup Strong Coffee
- Two tablespoons Sugar
- Two tablespoons Caramel Syrup
- Whipped Cream for garnish
- Caramel Syrup for garnish

## Instructions:

1. Add the milk into a smoothie maker or ice blender

2. Mix a caramel syrup with a coffee such that it's dissolved completely

3. Add the coffee to milk and blend to the consistency you like

4. Add ice, whipped cream and caramel syrup on top

# Conclusion

I'm very glad you've taken the time to read this book.

I hope that with regards to Fast food Copycat Recipes, all your questions are clear.

It is about learning the restaurants' simple ingredients and techniques to make the masterpiece dish to create a Copycat Recipe.

Creating a copy of the popular dish also allows you to adjust the ingredients used according to your tastes and health restrictions to produce a custom recipe.

It is also a cost-effective way to eat popular meals that you want. Keep cooking and try to work with the recipes.

Well, thanks and good luck!

CPSIA information can be obtained
at www.ICGtesting.com
Printed in the USA
BVHW061225010321
601386BV00001B/100